3 Strands, 1 Cord:
A Couple's Curriculum on Relationships and Reentry

3 Strands, 1 Cord:
A Couple's Curriculum on Relationships and Reentry

Better Halves United Publishing
Cleveland, Ohio

2023© Alfred & Roberta Cleveland
Better Halves United Publishing

ISBN#978-0-9845543-8-6

All rights reserved. No part of this workbook may be reproduced, distributed, or transmitted in any form or by any means, without prior permission of the publishers, except in the case of brief quotations or use of "Couple Exercises" for Relationship program purposes. For permission requests, contact cleve@youngchristianprofessionals.org

MISSION STATEMENT:

Our mission is to improve family bonds through the relationships of married and committed couples experiencing incarceration

Table of Contents

The 3 Strands, 1 Cord Relationship Course _____ 9
Overview _____ 12
Orientation _____ 14

LESSON 1
Relationship Number 1 _____ 18

LESSON 2
True Love _____ 23

LESSON 3
True Romance _____ 34

LESSON 4
True Friendship _____ 47

LESSON 5
Fools _____ 54

LESSON 6
Communication (Pt. 1) _____ 59

LESSON 7
Communication (Pt. 2) _____ 66

LESSON 8
True Heroes _____ 73

LESSON 9
Family _____ 79

LESSON 10
The Recipe _____ 86

3 Strands,
1 Cord

3 Strands, 1 Cord

The 3 Strands, 1 Cord Relationship Course

3 Strands, 1 Cord is a 10-week course for married and committed couples primarily in the institutional setting. Created by Alfred & Roberta Cleveland, a couple who has endured the conditions of incarceration for nearly 25 years, this program embodies the life lessons and biblical principles that have carried them through the concrete and razor wire circumstances of prison with grace.

Compelled by the belief that love, reconciliation, redemption, and restoration can take place in any relationship, the couple set out to produce a program that will help families and couples endure and persevere through their incarceration period, as well as increase one's general relationship skills. The Curriculum and Workbook will teach couples the following:

- how to do time together successfully
- what true love is according to biblical standards
- unique advantages to an incarcerated relationship
- how to improve friendships and relationships in general
- how to detect the little foxes that seek to destroy the relational vine
- how to handle court delays and denials
- how to overcome the negativity of family members and friends, and much, much more!

The 10-week course is designed to be taken in the prison environment by both couples (CFC). Because of particular restrictions and policies at certain institutions that may prevent couple interaction, the program is set up with an incarcerated-only model (CFI) as well.

Primary Model

1. **CFC (Course for Couples)** – The primary setting for which this program should take place is with couples in a designated meeting room area once per week where they will undergo the program's lessons and activities. Once per month could work if this is not feasible, but classes should be held once per week by the incarcerated group.

The most common place to accomplish this, in most cases, would be the facility's Chapel or Visiting Room areas while other places may have designated areas for such.

A Staff Advisor within the institution should be selected as a point person to handle all program logistics within the facility. Potential participants in the institution's general population will be informed of the program's starting date through the flier system unless otherwise promoted by the facility. Those interested will sign the flier and be passed for an orientation prior to the program's start date.

Secondary Model

2. CFI (Course for Inmates only) – In this alternative, the 10-week course will be administered to inmates only, who themselves will be responsible for sharing course information with their partners.

A designated area will be assigned for classes to be held. Potential participants in the facility's general population will be notified of the program's starting date by the flier system as well. Signees will be interviewed and selected.

Selected participants will be required to attend at least 80% of the classes, and complete at least 80% of the homeworks and exercises to graduate successfully. If participants do not meet this requirement, they may continue attending classes but will be unable to graduate and receive certification.

3 Strands, 1 Cord: A Couple's Curriculum on Relationships and Reentry

OVERVIEW

The following is a summary of the ten studies contained herein:

ORIENTATION
A date for the orientation shall be scheduled prior to the beginning of Week One to familiarize potential participants of the nature of the program and its requirements. This will be done through the program's Introduction, Ground Rules and Questionnaire in the Orientation section.

LESSON 1: "RELATIONSHIP NUMBER ONE"
This lesson acquaints participants with what we know to be the single most important relationship...God!

LESSON 2: "TRUE LOVE"
Designed to show us God's standard of love which we should strive to model. To also act as a mirror to show us where we are on the love scale, and how far we are from where we need to be.

LESSON 3: "TRUE ROMANCE"
Shows spouses and spouses-to-be how important doing little things for their partners are in a relationship, as well as helping them be creative in their thoughts and actions towards one another.

LESSON 4: "TRUE FRIENDSHIP"
Created to help couples better discern the friendships they have, and how to be better friends themselves.

LESSON 5: "FOOLS"
This lesson is designed to help participants better discern who they associate with and guard them against unhealthy relationships.

LESSON 6: "COMMUNICATION (Pt. 1)"
Helps couples communicate better under the unique circumstances of incarceration and afterwards.

LESSON 7: "COMMUNICATION (Pt. 2)"
Help couples understand the crucial component to maintaining a relationship during incarceration: Emotional Support.

LESSON 8: "TRUE HEROES"
This lesson helps couples understand what a Hero is, and how they have an opportunity, as Christians, to live the heroic life.

LESSON 9: "FAMILY"
This study highlights the traps, snares and steps seducers use to be cautious of.

LESSON 10: "THE RECIPE"
This expository teaching on Proverbs 31 highlights the ultimate industrious partner!

3 Strands, 1 Cord: A Couple's Curriculum on Relationships and Reentry

ORIENTATION

Introduction

Welcome to the *3 Strands, 1 Cord: Relationship and Reentry* Program! Our curriculum and workbook is designed for two specific purposes: to help couples enduring incarceration overcome the tremendous odds against them as well as help them overcome all unhealthy relationships!

Our hope for couples experiencing incarceration is that this program will help them unearth hidden truths about themselves and their partners that will empower them both through their journey of separation.

It's more than just a relationship course for couples. It's one that stretches and encourages participants to examine the quality of their relationships with their partners, family, friends, the community, and God.

As an eagle flies into the storm, using the winds to reach higher altitudes, this is a work that will help couples achieve greater intimacy through what may be their toughest storm in life. It will also help couples implement biblical truths into their relationships that will aid in unleashing the potential for love and longevity that God has given each and every one of us deep within.

So with the guidance of the Holy Spirit, join us as we travel at depths where life's most valuable pearls lie—a place where you and your partner can truly discover the essence of *3 Strands, 1 Cord!*

3 Strands, 1 Cord: A Couple's Curriculum on Relationships and Reentry

Ground Rules

1. It is highly recommended for couples doing the lesson together, to do one lesson at a time. Set a date and time after the classes to discuss the questions and answers on the phone. If phone availability is not an option, pick a day of the week you will both complete and send your responses to each other in the mail. (Avoid the temptation of receiving and reviewing your partners answers first before you complete and send yours. As with your relationship, honesty must be the basis of this course.)

2. Before you send your answers to your partner, make a copy of the lesson and send to them to fill out. A copy of the workbook can also be purchased on Amazon for $20 if your partner wishes to follow along.

3. Please be mindful of the program time limitations and keep your sharing and responses brief (no more than 2 minutes if possible). Others may want to share as well. We follow the 5 B's of sharing: "Be brief, brother, be brief."

4. Participants in group settings are required to direct their answers, responses, and comments, to group facilitators and advisors, not the other participants!

5. The concepts we share will not apply to every relationship, as circumstances in each relationship are wide and varied. Simply receive truths that work for you and apply them. Bypass what doesn't.

6. Three (3) or more absences will prohibit the participant from graduating.

7. All lessons and assignments are expected to be completed and turned in on time.

3 Strands, 1 Cord

LESSON 1:
Relationship Number One

3 Strands, 1 Cord: A Couple's Curriculum on Relationships and Reentry

LESSON 1:
Relationship Number 1

1. What is the #1 hindrance to forming good relationships?

2. What is the key method used in building good relationships?

3. In what ways do we do that (with those in here and out)?

_____   _____   _____

_____   _____   _____

4. What would you say is the most important relationship we can have?

5. What is this primary mode of communication?

Communication Exercise
"So let us come boldly to the throne of grace..." (Hebrews 4: 16)

What do you want?

What do you desire? What is your vision? What do you want most in this world? What do you want for your life? Don't be humble?

_____

_____

_____

_____

Prayer

Phil. 4: 6   _____

Col. 4: 2   _____

1Thess. 5: 16   _____

Lk. 11:24   _____

Jn. 14: 13   _____

Jn. 16: 23   _____

Mk. 11: 24   _____

What are the Keys?!

When you have this kind of heart, you count your blessings. This is the pipeline through which the favor of God flows. When we complain, we're just indicating to God that we're not content with what He has given us, which conveys _____

"Ears to hear and eyes to see—both are gifts from the Lord." (Proverbs 20: 12)

6. What do you have to be grateful for? _____

_____

7. Do you know what plays a big part of our ungratefulness? _____

8. What is Humility?

When someone is humble, they're focused on God and others. Even their focus on others is out of a desire to love and glorify God. They pray because they know they are dependent on and need God. They thank Him and others often. Whatever they receive is appreciated!

Notes

Notes

LESSON 2:
True Love

3 Strands, 1 Cord: A Couple's Curriculum on Relationships and Reentry

LESSON 2:
True Love

> "Love is patient and kind. Love is not jealous or boastful or proud or rude. It does not demand its own way. It is not irritable, and it keeps no record of being wronged. It does not rejoice about injustice, but rejoices whenever the truth wins out. Love never gives up, never loses faith, is always hopeful, and endures through every circumstance."
> ~ 1 Corinthians 13: 4-8 (NLT)

I. LOVE

1. "Love is patient..."

AMPLIFICATION: It is not easily irritated, angered, or quick-tempered. It fully accepts the character of their partners!

Breakdown: _____

- Free partner: Do you have what it takes to remain faithful to your partner while he is incarcerated?

- Imagine if God was irritated or quick-tempered with us every time we did something wrong. What kind of relationship would that produce?

2. "...and kind."

AMPLIFICATION: It's generous, graceful and looks for ways to add value to other people's lives.

Breakdown: _____

- Would your partner describe you as kind and generous?

3. "Love is not jealous…"

AMPLIFICATION: It is not envious, nor does it try to control their partners.

Breakdown: _____

- How does your partner respond when you share good news of a blessing you receive?

4. "…or boastful or proud or rude."

AMPLIFICATION: Love is not unmannerly. It respects others and is considerate of others feelings and belongings.

Breakdown: _____

- Incarcerated partner, do you feel respected by your free partner? If not, do you feel she would respect you more if you were out?

5. "It does not demand its own way."

AMPLIFICATION: It doesn't insist on its own rights or is self-seeking. It is concerned about and tries to fulfill the needs of their partners.

Breakdown: _____

- Are you frustrated with your partner when you don't get your way?

6. "It is not irritable and it keeps no record of being wronged."

AMPLIFICATION: Love takes no account of the evil done to it or pays attention to a suffered wrong. It doesn't dwell on past evils, and even destroys evidence of it when possible.

Breakdown: _____

- Are you dwelling on a past wrong your partner has committed that you said you forgave him/her of? Do you still find yourself bringing it up or throwing it in their face?

- Would you consider your partner hypersensitive about certain subjects?

7. "It does not rejoice about injustice. It rejoices whenever truth wins out. Love never gives up..."

AMPLIFICATION: Love bears up under anything and everything that comes.

Breakdown: _____

8. "...never loses faith..."

AMPLIFICATION: Love is ever ready to believe the best of every person. It believes in their partners without doubt.

Breakdown: _____

- Do you still believe in your partner?

9. "...is always hopeful..."

AMPLIFICATION: It's hopes are fadeless under all circumstances.

Breakdown: _____

10. "...and endures through every circumstance."

AMPLIFICATION: It is able to endure everything and every circumstance without weakening, even when the love is not reciprocated.

Breakdown: _____

- With this picture of love, can you say you truly love your partner on this level? If not, try to define, more accurately, your feelings for your partner.

HOMEWORK: Review, answer questions, then discuss with your partner.

EXERCISE FOR COUPLES

RELATIONSHIP REPORT CARD

This Relationship Report Card is simply designed to open communication, uncover profound insights, and provide a practical tool for change and improvement in relationships. Fill out the following by grading yourself, then your partner from A+ through F, just as you would on a school report card. Then discuss grades with your partner.

	YOURSELF	YOUR PARTNER
1. Affection		
2. Arguing Skills		
3. Attitude		
4. Commitment		
5. Considerate		
6. Couple Thinking		
7. Creativity		
8. Empathy		
9. Flexibility		
10. Friendship		
11. Generosity		
12. Gift-Giving Skills		
13. Honesty		
14. Household Mgt.		
15. Listening Skills		
16. Patience		
17. Playfulness		
18. Romance		
19. Self-Awareness		
20. Sense of Humor		
21. Sensitivity		
22. Spontaneity		
23. Tolerance		

3 Strands,
1 Cord

EXERCISE FOR COUPLES

RELATIONSHIP REPORT CARD

This Relationship Report Card is simply designed to open communication, uncover profound insights, and provide a practical tool for change and improvement in relationships. Fill out the following by grading yourself, then your partner from A+ through F, just as you would on a school report card. Then discuss grades with your partner.

	YOURSELF	YOUR PARTNER
1. Affection		
2. Arguing Skills		
3. Attitude		
4. Commitment		
5. Considerate		
6. Couple Thinking		
7. Creativity		
8. Empathy		
9. Flexibility		
10. Friendship		
11. Generosity		
12. Gift-Giving Skills		
13. Honesty		
14. Household Mgt.		
15. Listening Skills		
16. Patience		
17. Playfulness		
18. Romance		
19. Self-Awareness		
20. Sense of Humor		
21. Sensitivity		
22. Spontaneity		
23. Tolerance		

3 Strands,
1 Cord

Notes

Notes

LESSON 3:
True Romance

LESSON 3:
True Romance

> "Catch all the foxes, those little foxes, before they ruin the vineyard of love, for the grapevines are blossoming!"
> ~ Song of Solomon 2: 15

1. What is a Gentleman?

2. What is a Sweetheart?

3. What is Romance?

Romantics are like cheerleaders; they are the biggest fans of their partners. They provide enthusiastic support, constant encouragement, and unconditional love. They give little things; personal things; meaningful things; goofy things; comic strips, love quotes, flowers, cards, candy, magazine articles, little trinkets etc.

4. Can you share something romantic you've done for your partners in the past?

5. Who are Romantics?

- They are magnets for romantic ideas

- In society, they keep an eye on the concerts and shows that are scheduled to appear in the area that their partners like

- They read magazines and newspapers not only for the news, but for romantic ideas. Even in here, they go to the library, read them, make copies of interesting ones and send them

- They not only work at it, but they have fun doing it because it involves being creative, expressive, and they love being passionate

- Romantics live in the moment. "Carpe diem" – seize the day! Seize the moment. Don't let another day go by without making some expression of your love for your wife/partner

6. What do they do?

They pay attention to details. They give their relationship top priority. Everything else flows from the relationship, through the relationship, and because of the relationship. They support their partners and help each other grow.

- They wrap her gifts in her favorite color
- They don't buy her gold when she prefers silver
- They don't buy just any flowers – they get her favorites

By the way, did you know that different color roses have different meanings?

- Red roses = _____
- Pink roses = _____
- Yellow roses = _____
- White roses = _____

In romance, the receiver defines what's romantic. For example, if you give her flowers, and she hates flowers, it's not romantic.

TIPS:

- For incarcerated partners, if your wife/partner loves flowers and you don't have the means to have any sent, have a botanical painting or drawing done with a poem, quote, or message you wrote put on it. They make great gifts for the kitchen or her workplace. (where she can see it every day)

- Learn how to make paper flowers, or wooden ones

- Send flattened flowers. They're great for bookmarks and you can send them in the mail

- Or if you have the means, have a family member order from 1-800-FLOWERS; 1-800-580-2913 (proflowers); 1-800-SEND-FTD. (Always ask for fresh ones. A good, fresh rose should last a week. An older one can wilt in a day.)

> - There are many other gifts you can make or have made in prison, like jewelry boxes, doll houses, ships, cars, drawings, portraits, dogs, birds, books, magazine subscriptions, shoes, jewelry, bibles, video-cards, poetry etc.

CREATIVE TIPS FOR YOUR LOVE LETTERS AND POEMS

- Write them on nice parchment paper
- Turn them into scrolls, tied with ribbon
- Frame 'em
- Have them rendered in calligraphy
- Publish your love letters in a book
- Place a love note in the classified section of a newspaper
- Create a poster of a famous poem or one you wrote

7. Read Song of Solomon, Chapter 7

8. Are these two in love? If so, how do you know?

9. What are some terms used in the language of love?

VALUABLE DON'TS AS A GENTLEMAN:

- Don't throw it in her face when you're right
- Don't let her carry heavy packages. You carry them
- Don't let her open the car door when you can open it for her
- Don't make the same mistake twice
- Don't undermine your partner's authority with your kids
- Don't hold grudges
- Don't let your mind wander during conversations
- Don't take her for granted
- Don't reveal the end of a movie
- Don't be so judgmental
- Don't spend your prime time watching TV (use a Recorder)
- Don't just sign, "Love" on your cards. Be eloquent

- Don't wait. Carpe' diem! Express your love today through email system, letter, or phone!

HOMEWORK: Review lesson, answer questions, then discuss with your partner.
EXERCISE: Complete the "How Well Do You Know Your Partner" handout. Send one to your partner and discuss.

Common Literary Tools
for Writing Love Letters, Poems, and Other Romantic Endeavors

Simile – involves explicit comparison of two unlike things using "as" or "like."
"Her eyes are like doves" = means her eyes are soft and beautiful
"She's like a lily among thorns" = means she's a beautiful sight in the midst of unsightly things

Parables – An extended Simile

Metaphors – involves a direct or implied comparison of two unlike things
"The sound of her voice was music to my ears" = means the way she spoke was very pleasing
"He is my shield, the power that saves me, and my place of safety" (2Sam. 22: 3)

Personification – a figure of speech which takes on a human characteristic and applies it to an object, quality, or idea
"The streets are watching" = means people are paying close attention to a situation
"The beautiful house we saw spoke to us" = houses can't speak. It appealed to the couple strongly

Hyperbole – where the writer exaggerates to create a strong effect
"I write the songs that make the whole world sing" = means his songs make people happy. The whole world couldn't possibly hear all his songs.
"All the women love him, his name is like a fragrance among them" = all women couldn't love him because all women don't know him. He is just a very attractive man.

Metonomy – In metonomy, the name of one object or concept is used for another because of an association or similarity between the two.
"I saved 5 stacks" = stacks is a word for thousand

Euphemism – A euphemistic figure substitutes an inoffensive or agreeable expression for one that may offend or suggest something distasteful
"Whoever hates me loves death" = No one loves death. To hate God is to hate life

Litotes – involves belittling or the use of a negative statement to affirm a truth
"I'm just a pea in a pod" = means I'm not as important to you
"It's your world, I'm just living in it." = means you're the boss

Synecdoche – In a synecdoche, a part is used as a whole, or a whole as part
"Lord, guide my feet" = feet means actions; path
"For God so loved the world" = "World" is used for people in the world

3 Strands,
1 Cord

EXERCISE:

HOW WELL DO YOU KNOW YOUR PARTNER?

Fill out this questionnaire and discuss the answers with your partner.
If your partner is not part of the class, send a copy to her/him and share your thoughts.

1. What is your favorite food?	26. Favorite author?
2. Fast food?	27. Favorite clothes color?
3. Restaurant?	28. What animal would you be?
4. Favorite Vegetable?	29. Favorite season?
5. Fruit?	30. Favorite holiday?
6. TV Show?	31. Favorite time of the day?
7. Favorite movie?	32. Favorite day of week?
8. Favorite romance movie?	33. Favorite cologne/perfume?
9. Favorite book?	34. Favorite grocery store?
10. Favorite Actor?	35. Favorite clothing store?
11. Actress?	36. Favorite clothing designer?
12. Favorite scripture?	37. Favorite shoe store?
13. Favorite book in the Bible?	38. Favorite tennis shoe brand?
14. Favorite color?	39. Favorite feature of your body?
15. Favorite song?	40. Your partner's?
16. Favorite CD?	41. Favorite kind of jewelry?
17. Favorite music genre?	42. Favorite ice cream?
18. Favorite love song?	43. Favorite subject in school?
19. Favorite number?	44. Favorite cartoon character?
20. Favorite car?	45. Favorite way to relax?
21. Favorite SUV?	46. Favorite instrument?
22. Favorite athlete?	47. Favorite magazine?
23. Favorite sport to play?	48. Favorite flower/plant?
24. To watch?	49. Favorite city?
25. Favorite hobby?	50. Favorite car color?

3 Strands, 1 Cord

EXERCISE:

HOW WELL DO YOU KNOW YOUR PARTNER?

Fill out this questionnaire and discuss the answers with your partner.
If your partner is not part of the class, send a copy to her/him and share your thoughts.

1. What is your favorite food?	26. Favorite author?
2. Fast food?	27. Favorite clothes color?
3. Restaurant?	28. What animal would you be?
4. Favorite Vegetable?	29. Favorite season?
5. Fruit?	30. Favorite holiday?
6. TV Show?	31. Favorite time of the day?
7. Favorite movie?	32. Favorite day of week?
8. Favorite romance movie?	33. Favorite cologne/perfume?
9. Favorite book?	34. Favorite grocery store?
10. Favorite Actor?	35. Favorite clothing store?
11. Actress?	36. Favorite clothing designer?
12. Favorite scripture?	37. Favorite shoe store?
13. Favorite book in the Bible?	38. Favorite tennis shoe brand?
14. Favorite color?	39. Favorite feature of your body?
15. Favorite song?	40. Your partner's?
16. Favorite CD?	41. Favorite kind of jewelry?
17. Favorite music genre?	42. Favorite ice cream?
18. Favorite love song?	43. Favorite subject in school?
19. Favorite number?	44. Favorite cartoon character?
20. Favorite car?	45. Favorite way to relax?
21. Favorite SUV?	46. Favorite instrument?
22. Favorite athlete?	47. Favorite magazine?
23. Favorite sport to play?	48. Favorite flower/plant?
24. To watch?	49. Favorite city?
25. Favorite hobby?	50. Favorite car color?

3 Strands, 1 Cord

Notes

Notes

LESSON 4:
True Friendship

3 Strands, 1 Cord: A Couple's Curriculum on Relationships and Reentry

LESSON 4:
True Friendship

> "A friend is always loyal..."
> ~Proverbs 17: 17

I. FRIEND

1. What is a friend? _____

_____

2. What is Trust? Firm reliance in the honesty, dependability, strength, or character of someone

II. FRIENDSHIP

1. 1Samuel 18: 1-9; 20: 1-4

2. Does Jonathan possess the qualities of a true friend?

III. EXAMINING FRIEND TYPES

Aside from character issues, many of us fail at having real friendships because of a lack of effort (as we discussed in lesson 1), and we don't have a clear understanding of the various levels of friendships and their responsibilities and freedoms. Oftentimes, one person feels the friendship is one thing, while the other person feels it to be another. So to bring greater clarity, listed below are a few general levels.

1. Acquaintance – A person whom one knows and has general conversation with.

2. Associate – A casual friendship that is usually based on common interests or endeavors. These friends go a little deeper, asking specific questions, expressing different ideas, or talking about goals with each other.

3. Close Friendship – These friendships are based on similar goals in life. Aspirations, plans, and dreams, especially as they relate to working together, are commonly expressed at this level.

4. True Friend (Best Friends) – At this level, the friends share openly at a deep level, and strive to help each other develop inner qualities. These friends have your best interest at heart. They are confidants, and will correct you if needed. Can you think of people in your lives that would fit these categories?

IV. FRIENDS: A CLOSER LOOK

1. [1]Period Friendships – Oftentimes, these are friendships we form with those we do time with. In the world, they may be those who are a part of the same movement, team, company, organization, and in some cases, ministry team. They have common interests, and this commonality creates a cohesiveness between the friends based on the common goals.

There usually appears to be an added zeal to the friendship, and this behavior can make one believe there is love and loyalty in the relationship when nothing may be further from the truth. The trouble with this type of friend is that while a genuine friendship appears to have been developed, this type of friend is only a friend of what they're doing together. In other words, they're "friends of the cause."

- Since your incarceration, can you classify any of your relationships as "period friendships"? Explain.

- Could the relationship with your partner be a "period relationship"?

2. Mutual Friendships – These are friendships based on the mutual advantages one has with the other. When one is unable or not willing to contribute to the relationship as he/she once did, the relationship begins to fade.

---

[1] Smith, Fred. 1984. You and Your Network. W Pub Group

Everyone would like to believe their friends are genuine friends, and not with them for money, resources, access, status, or what you are doing for them. But quite often, time reveals the relational motives.

- Looking back, were any of your relationships based on mutual advantage? If so, explain.

V. ENEMIES TO THE RELATIONSHIP

1. SNAKES

Knowing you are away now, some individuals whom you thought were friends you may find out have been secretly coveting your spouse/partner for years, and may now seek to strike the relationship at what seems its weakest point.

Surreptitiously, they may stop by your partner's house in an attempt to penetrate the relationship, posing as if they want to help your partner in your absence, perhaps financially or otherwise. They may even offer to drive your partner around to run errands or take them to the prison to see you. Or, even better, they may offer to help with work around the house.

> *Cathy Tijerina, co-founder of TYRO, tells of an encounter in a book she co-authored, about her husband's "friend," who came by after her husband was sent to prison.*
>
> *After cautiously opening her door and seeing the "friend" there alone, he asked how her children were doing and if he could come inside. Since Ron was in prison, he stood on the step with a smile on his face, explaining that he could help her "in any way she needed." Cathy's stomach turned at his audacity, thinking he could come to their home and prey on her grief and exploit Ron's absence. She looked him in the eye and told him it was her policy to never let a man in her home alone. And with an incredulous look, he reminded her that her husband would be gone for a very long time. "Exactly," she stated. "You may come back when he is home."*

- Do you have friends you thought were friends, but found out were "snakes" according to the description in the above scenario? Who?

- Do you have friends you consider true friends? If so, please list them.

CONCLUSION: In your quiet time, reflect and begin to evaluate the friendships you presently have in your life, as well as those in your past. If you have not been a good friend, repent for the friendships you've destroyed or the people you've hurt specifically, and ask God for forgiveness. Decide from this day forward to be an honest friend.

What is the key to attracting true friends?

HOMEWORK: Review lesson, answer questions, send copy to your partner, then discuss

Notes

Notes

LESSON 5:
Fools

LESSON 5:
Fools

"...associate with fools and get in trouble."
~ Proverbs 13:20

1. Associate – to join in a relationship

2. Fool – one deficient in good sense or judgment.

3. Discernment – the ability to perceive something hidden or obscure

- Has associating with a fool ever gotten you in trouble? If so, who?

I. The Biblical Fool – Exposed

1. Who is he? He is not someone lacking intellectually, but he is _____

& _____.

2. Who does Jesus call the fool?

Verse	Breakdown
_____ –	_____
_____ –	_____
_____ –	_____
_____ –	_____
_____ –	_____

_____ — _____
_____ — _____
_____ — _____
_____ — _____
_____ — _____
_____ — _____
_____ — _____
_____ — _____
_____ — _____
_____ — _____
_____ — _____
_____ — _____
_____ — _____
_____ — _____
_____ — _____

3. Read Matthew 5: 21-22. What does Jesus say about calling people fools (idiots)?

Conclusion: If you discern these characteristics in a "friend" or associate, proceed with extreme caution. It is best to keep them at a distance, or cut ties altogether. What does oil have to do with water?

Notes

Notes

3 Strands, 1 Cord: A Couple's Curriculum on Relationships and Reentry

LESSON 6:
Communication (Pt.1)

LESSON 6:
Communication (Pt.1)

I. LOYALTY

1. What is Loyalty? _____

   • If one tells you they're loyal, does that mean they are?

   • What about love, can words prove that?

2. Commitment – _____

   • In marriage vows, what does "For better or for worse" mean to you?

   • Besides incarceration, can you think of situations besides incarceration that might put that to the test?

In order to be successful as a partner under any of these conditions, one must remember the commitment and the good times, and understand that disasters and tragedies can cause one of two things to happen: You either grow closer to each other, or you decide you are not going to be a sacrificial lamb and jump ship.

3. Read Ruth 1: 1-17 together.

- Is Noemi loyal?

II. NEGATIVE COMMUNICATION

1. What kind of partner should you avoid? _____

III. NOT LISTENING

- What are some reasons some men don't listen to women?

1. The barrier you must overcome to discovering a woman's goldmine of treasure is

_____. Seek to first _____, before

being _____.

> "The husband must fulfill his wife's sexual needs,
> and the wife should fulfill her husband's"
> ~ 1Cor. 7: 3

In a conversation, one might find out his/her views are totally different on a given topic. Without trying to probe deeper into why or what led their belief in this, we march forward with our views and positions in an effort to persuade or conform. If they are strong-minded and sticks to their guns, this may sow discord and a disagreement that can lead to an all-out fight. This can be avoided if partners learn to listen actively and seek to UNDERSTAND their partner.

Ask yourself:

- What makes him/her believe what they believe?
- Who in his/her life influenced them growing up?

- What are his/her parent's values and beliefs?
- What experiences has he/she had that led her to say what she said?

IV. ACTIVE LISTENING & INTERRUPTING

1. What is Active Listening?

Active listening is listening with sincere concern for what someone is saying to gain a greater understanding of the person and what they are saying. It is listening with empathy; without judgment; and not with the intent of rebutting for the sake of rebutting.

It is listening with love. (Ephesians 4: 2) It is listening with the intent to learn.

2. What happens when you really listen? It brings_____, _____, _____ and _____.

If you have a disagreement or argument with your partner, before you make up your mind to "set her straight because she's dead wrong on the issue," take time to understand, and listen with love.

3. INTERRUPTING. Are you an interrupter? Interrupting is not a habit many of us are aware of. Those who do are often frustrating to talk with.

- Do you INTERRUPT?
  Interrupters interrupt or make comments while the other partner is still talking.

- Do you TALK OVER people?

- Do you TALK FOR people?

If you are any of these, learn how to _____ and let people complete their sentences before you respond. This conveys love and respect! Be patient, be gentle, and speak in love.

3 Strands, 1 Cord: A Couple's Curriculum on Relationships and Reentry

V. "WHY" QUESTIONS

According to Tony Stoltzfuz in his Coaching Questions Manual, "Why" questions tend to make people clam up, because it challenges motives. When you pose a question like, "Why did you do that?" you are asking your partner to defend and justify their actions. So don't be surprised if she gets defensive!

SOLUTION:_____

> EXAMPLE:
> - Why didn't you come when you told me you were?
>   *Better: What happened that you were not able to come?*
> - Why didn't you answer the phone last night?
>   *Better:* _____
> - Why'd you come home so late?
>   *Better:* _____
> - Why didn't you send the food box?
>   *Better:* _____

CONCLUSION: Think more before you say things to your partner, and remember to say what you need to say IN LOVE.

HOMEWORK: Review lesson, answer questions, send copy to your partner, then discuss.
EXERCISE: Begin "Crossword Puzzle" questions

Notes

Notes

3 Strands, 1 Cord: A Couple's Curriculum on Relationships and Reentry

LESSON 7:
Communication (Pt. 2)

3 Strands, 1 Cord: A Couple's Curriculum on Relationships and Reentry

LESSON 7:
Communication (Pt. 2)

I. PHONE TONE

Have you ever said something to your partner during a conversation that you knew was right and truthful, only to find out there has been a sudden shift in the overall mood? In your innermost thoughts, you go back, reflect, and replay the conversation and cannot for the life of you figure out what went wrong. You can tell things are not right by the distant attitude. Well fellas, welcome to the penitentiary doghouse!

This doghouse is located on the couch of voice-mails and/or dry and stale conversations. This can be caused by a number of things, but another little fox you have to watch out for is the TONE in which you said the thing.

Though what you said may be correct and normally helpful, you may have said it...

_____

_____

_____

_____

Example: She overslept and missed taking your son/daughter to a soccer (or baseball) game. You "check" her for that, because she should know better.

- She might not say anything, but what might her thoughts be?

- Read Luke 6: 42 (Take out "friend" and, for men, replace with "woman." For women, replace with "man.")

- Has anyone ever told you a truth about yourself that was dead on, but you didn't receive it because of the way they said it?

Solution: _____

II. FACTS & MEANINGS

This sly little fox often breeds misunderstanding, confusion, and undue stress. The following is an example from Tim Muelhoff's, *I Beg to Differ*, where the misinterpretation of facts and meanings can hurt relationships.

At one of his speeches, President Obama, while on the campaign trail, didn't wear his lapel pin and his opponents pointed this out in the media, accusing him of being unpatriotic.

- The fact is_____.

- The meaning was_____.

Meanings can have various interpretations.

What if you had an argument with your partner on a visit concerning a difficult issue? When your visits are usually over, you go back and call her to confirm the great visit you had, tell her you love her, and see if she made it home alright. But this time, the phone goes directly to voice-mail. What would you think?

The facts are_____

The meaning is_____

All stemmed from a _____

Solution: _____

III. EMOTIONAL SUPPORT

1. As humans, what must we do to grow physically?_____.

2. How do we grow mentally?_____.

3. Spiritually_____.

4. But how does one grow emotionally?_____.

> *When I was a young boy, I was leaving my friend's house next door, when their feisty little Chihuahua bit me on the leg, leaving the fang marks of Dracula. Blood dripping, I ran home and showed my mother who became angry that my friend's father had allowed this to happen. We both waited for my father to get home who we knew would head over there and "set him straight."*
>
> *When my father got home I anxiously watched as my mother told him of the incident in that tone used by a woman to galvanize a man to action. Anticipating what was about to happen, I snuck outside to get a front row seat at what was about to occur. As expected, my father walked out the house and into the neighbor's backyard where he stood there talking with the man in front of his garage.*
>
> *After a few minutes, my father uneventfully emerged and calmly told me to go in the house. What transpired during that conversation I don't know, but I'm sure the neighbor convinced my father that the vicious Chihuahua attack was not done maliciously, and I even thought I saw them chuckling, probably at the size of the little dog. In any event, days later, my friend's dad apologized to me and all was well."*

It is through these relationships that we learn how to respond, behave, converse, befriend, and support one another. This is an area most incarcerated men are immature in.

- What do you think is the primary reason for this?

- In the above scenario, what if I had no father in my life and watched my angry mother go over there and threaten the man with violence?

- Read Proverbs 22: 24-25. ("Don't befriend angry people or associate with hot-tempered people, or you will be like them and endanger your soul.")

As babies, we are not born into this world angry. Anger is a learned behavior. It's transferred.

Homework: (1-2 page essay) Was there a particular moment in your life where you became angry?

Notes

Notes

3 Strands, 1 Cord: A Couple's Curriculum on Relationships and Reentry

LESSON 8:
True Heroes

LESSON 8:
True Heroes

1. What is a Hero? – _____

   • Who are your heroes?

2. Read Luke 10: 30-37.

   • Is there a hero in this story? If so, why?

Four qualities heroes share:

REALNESS – He is not myth or fantasy, or superhero. They are not perfect, but real people with flaws.

DEDICATED – They live with a purpose and die for a cause bigger than them.

CONCENTRATION – They have the ability to think the right thing at the right time. This requires poise and mental discipline in the face of opposition.

SACRIFICE – They sacrifice their talents, time or lives for those who look up to them. They will be remembered not for what they got, but for what they gave. They are responsible. Not the "I'm a do-me" generation.

---

3. Are there any heroes in your life?

4. Read Matthew 25: 34-40.

- Can any of these be considered heroes?

- Christianity is _____

We cannot live fully without heroes, for they are the stars to guide us upward. They are the peaks on our human mountains. Not only do they personify what we can be, but they also urge us to be.

Heroes are those who have changed history for the better. They are not always the men and women of highest potential, but those who have exploited their potential on society's behalf. Their deeds are done not for the honor, but for the duty. Through our study of heroes we enter the realities of greatness.

Heroes are the personification of our ideals, the embodiment of our highest values. A society writes its diary by naming its heroes. We as individuals do the same. When Socrates said, "Talk young man, that I might know you," he could have added, "Talk of your heroes that I might know not only who you are, but who you will become."

5. Who are some of America's heroes?

The real heroes are our partners who stick with us; the volunteers; YOU if you put service and OTHERS before you! And we have the greatest example of that that the world has ever seen!

7. Who is the greatest hero of all time?_____.

- He was a mere carpenter
- His very birth split time in half
- He is the central figure to the entire human race
- He had powers to heal the sick, open the eyes of the blind, cast out demons and bring death back to life, yet he never used His powers for Himself!
- He stood up to the system
- He forgave the chief haters in His life, even the ones that were killing Him
- He was the most righteous person that ever lived
- He took a case for us that we were absolutely guilty of.
- He came down from Glory, put himself in harm's way, and sacrificed his life for you and me so we could be saved
- The Bible says He is the King of all Kings, and Lord of all Lords, and He came through and saved humanity from eternal consequences, and eternal death. Now that's a HERO!

HOMEWORK: Review this lesson, answer the questions, then discuss answers with your partner. Hand in next week.

Notes

Notes

3 Strands, 1 Cord: A Couple's Curriculum on Relationships and Reentry

WEEK 9:
Family

3 Strands, 1 Cord: A Couple's Curriculum on Relationships and Reentry

WEEK NINE:
Family

OBJECTIVE: This study examines the history, enemies and threats to the family structure.

I. FAMILY

1. Function - (Webster's) _____

_____

_____

2. Family - (Webster's) A social unit consisting of parents and their offspring; 2) A group of people sharing a common ancestry; 3) All members of a household.

(Nelson's Bible Dictionary) - _____

_____

> [2]Family is the primary social unit within our society. Within the family, individuals are socialized, protected and nurtured so they can develop the skills necessary for their well-being and survival. To meet the needs of the individual, the family unit must first have its needs met.
>
> The basic family structure was the *Extended Family System*.

3. *Extended Family System* - Large families consisting of several generations including brothers, sisters, aunts, uncles, great aunts and uncles, all working closely together and living in close proximity to one another. (Anybody come from one of these families?) They needed to be large, because larger meant more available producers, and more producers meant the family was better off. When family problems occurred, the response was mutual aid within the extended family structure.

4. Nuclear Family - Usually consists of man, wife, and one or more children.

---
[2] Johnson, Louise. *Social Welfare: A response to Human Need.* Allyn & Bacon. Boston 1997

In the 70's variations of this type emerged:

- <u>Single Parent Family</u> - Formed by out-of-wedlock births, desertion, separation, divorce, death, or incarceration

- <u>Step Family</u> - (or Blended Family) Created when one or both partners in a marriage bring with them children from a former relationship

- <u>Cohabitation without Marriage</u> - Children can be present

5. What is the function of the family?

- To teach members the physical, social, intellectual, and emotional skills necessary to prepare them for membership into the larger society

- Help individuals through life cycle: marriage, birth of child, adolescence, child separating from family unit.

- To be in relationship that will create loving relationships

6. What role have you played in the family? Have you worked to build it up or tear it down? (Proverbs 11:29)

II. A DEEPER LOOK

A. FAMILY/COMMUNITY DESTROYERS

1. What is a Predator? - _____

_____

B. MARKS OF A PREDATOR

- They are irresponsible and self-centered. These individuals think everybody else is a fool. They're reckless and hurt people, and never learn from their mistakes because it's not their faults. They're accident prone, but its really that they never follow the rules.

- War Stories - They always brag about their wrongdoing - stuff normal people would find appalling. They thrive on outsmarting people, and view them as suckers. They do things just to get away with it.

- They lack Empathy - They don't feel the pain of others. They only think about themselves. They can steal a car or break into a home without considering the feeling of the victim. They can sell drugs and destroy human life, but only think about their pockets. They're promoting crime by selling to users who commit crimes to buy drugs

- Always Seeking an Advantage - They lie, cheat and steal. They seek an advantage, not a relationship. They always scheme.

- They're Manipulators - (con artists) They use flattery to get in with you (Proverbs 26: 28; 29: 5; 20: 19). They know that humans tend to like those that like them. They laugh at all your jokes, agree with all your positions and supports your efforts.

C. What is Anti-social behavior? _____

- Deceitful
- Very Impulsive)
- Extremely Irresponsible
- Financially Irresponsible
- Shows Little Remorse
- Irritable & Aggressive
- Inflated and Arrogant Self-Appraisal

D. How can one break this cycle?

"For in Christ lives all the fullness of God in a human body. So you also are complete through your union with Christ, who is the head over every ruler and authority.

When you came to Christ, you were circumcised, but not by a physical procedure. Christ performed a spiritual circumcision - cutting away of your sinful nature. For you were buried with Christ when you were baptized. And with Him you were raised to new life because you trusted the mighty power of God, who raised Christ from the dead.

You were dead because of your sins and because of your sinful nature was not yet cut away. Then God made you alive with Christ, for He forgave all our sins. He canceled the record of the charges against us and took it away by nailing it to the cross. In this way, he disarmed the spiritual rulers and authorities. He shamed them publicly by His victory over them on the cross."

~ Col. 2: 9-15) NLT

HOMEWORK: Review this lesson, answer the questions, then discuss answers with your partner.

Notes

Notes

WEEK TEN:
The Recipe

3 Strands, 1 Cord: A Couple's Curriculum on Relationships and Reentry

WEEK TEN:
The Recipe

OBJECTIVE: This expository teaching on Proverbs 31 highlights the ultimate industrious partner!

I. GODLY WOMAN

1. (v. 10) "Who can find a virtuous and capable wife? She is more precious than rubies."

"Virtuous" (Webster's) – One of moral excellence; an example of moral excellence.
"Capable" (Webster's) – Having ability or capacity; efficient. 2. Qualified.
AMPLIFICATION: A good woman is hard to find because they are scarce.
Breakdown: Her beautiful character is worth more than her physical beauty.

- Have you ever had a good woman in your life?

2. (v.11) "Her husband can trust her, and she will greatly enrich his life."

AMPLIFICATION: He fully trusts his wife because she has given him no reason to think she has been unfaithful.

Breakdown: _____

- Does your woman give you reasons to mistrust her? Do you?

3. (v. 12) "She brings him good, not harm, all the days of her life."

"Good" in Heb. "Tob" – Pleasure; desirable; prosperity; joy; kindness.
"Harm" in Heb. "Ra" – Hurt; wickedness; mischief; trouble; displeasure.
AMPLIFICATION: She constantly wants to do him good, even unconsciously.

Breakdown: "...all the days of her life."

4. (v. 13) "She finds wool and flax and busily spins it."

AMPLIFICATION: She looks for good, quality material at a good price.

Breakdown: She's industrious, hard-working and diligent. She delights in clothing her family in good, quality clothes. She loves what she does, and does it willingly.

5. (v. 14) "She is like a merchant's ship bringing her food from afar."

AMPLIFICATION: She shops around for bargains like a merchant ship travels from port to port to trade goods.

Breakdown: _____

- Is your partner good with money? Is she better with finances than you?

6. (v.15) "She gets up before dawn to prepare breakfast for her household and plan the day's work for her servant girls."

AMPLIFICATION: Her household is top priority!
Breakdown: She may even have a job in today's world, but she still rises early to make sure everybody is well-fed and equipped to take on the world.

7. (v. 16) "She goes to inspect a field and buys it; with her earnings she plants a vineyard."

"Inspect" or "Considers" in Heb. "Zamam" – determines; plans; intends; purposes.
AMPLIFICATION: She does her research and due diligence before investing her resources.

Breakdown: _____

- If you had the funds, would you trust your partner to make a sound investment?

8. (v. 17) "She is energetic and strong, a hard worker."

AMPLIFICATION: She does what she does with all her might.

Breakdown: She's all in, not half-hearted, and she's a hard worker, meaning, she'll get her hands dirty. She'll get on her hands and knees and scrub that floor.

9. (v. 18) "She makes sure her dealings are profitable; her lamp burns late into the night."

AMPLIFICATION: She will put in extra hours.
Breakdown: When she gets off work, she'll put in more hours to make sure her investment is paying off.

- If you and your partner invested in something, do you think she will put in the extra hours needed to make it successful?

10. (v. 20) "She extends a helping hand to the poor and opens her arms to the needy."

AMPLIFICATION: She is serious about giving.

Breakdown: _____

11. (v. 21) "She has no fear of winter for her household for everyone has warm clothes."

AMPLIFICATION: She dresses her family warmly.

Breakdown: _____

- Did your mother make sure you were dressed properly in the winter?

12. (v. 22) "She makes her own bedspreads. She dresses in fine linen and purple gowns."

AMPLIFICATION: She wears what she wears like royalty. (Not in rank or position)

Breakdown: _____

13. (v. 23) "Her husband is well known at the city gates, where he sits with other civic leaders."

AMPLIFICATION: Her husband is known because of his intelligence. (How do we know he's intelligent? Because he married her!)

Breakdown: He's respected for who he is, but also because of how her and his family reflects him.

- What do you think, "...known in the city gates" mean?

14. (v.25) "She is clothed with strength and dignity and she laughs without fear of the future."

AMPLIFICATION: Because of her righteousness and faith, she looks forward to the day Jesus returns; not fears it.

Breakdown: _____

15. (v.26) "When she speaks, her words are wise, and she gives instructions with kindness."

AMPLIFICATION: She gives her family sound counsel and guidance. They receive it, because they know she has their best interest at heart.

Breakdown: _____

HOMEWORK: NONE!

MAY GOD BLESS YOU AND YOUR FAMILIES!!

Dear Friend,

Congratulations on completing the *3 Strands, 1 Cord* Curriculum and Workbook!

We pray that some things about yourself were revealed that you can work on and other things were revealed about others that will help you make better decisions about who you allow in your life. Our relationships are extremely important to God. It's so important that you will be sure to find yourself and your partner under attack from the enemy of relationships, Satan, as you move forward. Perhaps you've been experiencing it throughout the program. If so, then you already understand how important this program is.

Our most important weapon against this is prayer, fighting back in the spiritual realm, on our knees in high places. So stay prayed up, every day and every night. Pray with your spouse, your partner, and keep God at the center and forefront and you will defeat the enemy and overcome his evil schemes and tactics. The victory has already been won, the crown is already yours, you just have to put it on and wear it. Jesus did the work so we can have a relationship with Him, and from that will flow the goodness of God through you to others!

God bless you all as you move forward into the next chapter in your lives and may you find the peace that surpasses all understanding on your journey forward, building successful and fruitful relationships with all you encounter!

With Love,

Alfred & Roberta Cle—
Alfred & Roberta Cleveland

3 Strands, 1 Cord: A Couple's Curriculum on Relationships and Reentry

YoungChristianProfessionals.org

PROVEN RESULTS FOR YOUNG ADULTS

8-WEEK CURRICULUM THAT DEVELOPS CHARACTER AND EXECUTIVE ETIQUETTE SKILLS

Made in United States
Orlando, FL
04 August 2024